An Educ (Online) Dating

Written By
Gary Gunn & Daniel De Haan

The online dating guide for the modern man in the cyber century

Copyright © Social Attraction Ltd 2016

All rights reserved. No part of this book may be produced, stored in a retrieval system, or transmitted in any form or by any means electronic, mechanical, photocopying recording, or otherwise without the prior permission of the authors or their publishers.

Copyright © Social Attraction Ltd. 2016

About The Authors

Gary Gunn is the founder of the Social Attraction Academy. He specialises in coaching single men how to meet and attract their ideal long term partner.

Daniel De Hann is an award winning screen writer. His background in film and TV production enables him to create the perfect role for any online dating character.

In their spare time the two of them can usually be found coaching the next generation of sporting stars across the south coast of England.

If you wish to correspond with the authors then please feel free to contact them direct at:

info@socialattraction.co.uk

www.socialattraction.co.uk

From Us To You

We wanted to take this opportunity to thank you for buying a copy of our book.

As a personal gesture, we have decided to provide you with a lifetime free support system by setting-up a brand new Facebook group titled:

"An Education In Online Dating"

Open to all, all you have to do is find us on Facebook, add yourself and you'll be able to post any questions about online dating and await our response…

In loving memory of Martin Culverhouse,
the kind of client first books are written about…

Foreword – An Interview With The Authors

"Yeah, why not!" the voice said rather energetically lighting up the line. It sounded unlike so many of my other dispassionate, monotone leads that I'd been trying best to cold call and tick off the list since I started this study. But this voice, this voice was different and now it was time to put a face to a name.

Attraction coach and all-round dating guru Gary Gunn was one of the most energetic and entertaining guys I'd witnessed whilst embarking on a research project into the changing of the communication age and how it affects attraction in the twenty first century.

Between the various YouTube clips and articles based around dating on his fledging website 'Social Attraction', I watched how he guided the fate of countless single guys lost and looking for love that had turned to him in the hope of having somewhere to go when truth be told, they didn't.

The night before we were to meet, I'd gone through my ritual, the same ritual I'd always put in place before I'd interview a subject matter of mine. Pen and pad…check. Dictaphone…check. Quotes, sources and subject material…check. After all, unlike that young energetic voice I'd spoken to just 48 hours before, I was old school so I knew what was expected of me. What I never expected however was that for the first time in my professional life, that checklist of mine wouldn't be.

"We good to go?" That same energetic voice said to me with a smile. And we were; only this time rather than being just a voice on the other end of the line, instead he was staring back at me. All 5ft10 and 150 pounds of him compacted into a former athlete's frame with a pop idol's hairstyle to match. I stared down at the red record button on my Dictaphone, my head telling my body to press play and yet for whatever reason, it wasn't.

"You need a moment?" he easily enquired. Yes was my first thought, no was my second as my ego kicked up a sudden fuss. There I was with over 15 years experience as an expert and leading psychotherapist, having psychoanalysed countless others and here I was being psychoanalysed back. The man had stolen my move.

More important than getting it back mind, was what he had to say for himself. Gary told me he was currently in the process of co-writing a book at the time with the working title, '*An Education in (Online) Dating*'. That afternoon it was to take a whole other course as we were both about to find out.

Listening to words I never thought I'd hear from a man of that age *(Gary had just turned 29 at the time)*, he spoke with such passion and such clarity about capturing a feeling of a generation, telling not just the story of one man but the story of so many young men of his time. Instinctively he spoke of people's need to be together raising the question again and again, is anybody truly wanting to be single anymore?

"I mean I'd tell you yes, but if you ask Dan he'd tell you differently, its more a matter of opinion depending on the way you see the world", he said sat matter-of-factly in answer to the question.

Rarely one to ever ask a question without knowing the answer, this time I had no choice, "Dan?" my face now a question mark. "My best kept secret or rather he tells me to call him that when people ask". And then there were three...

"This is the age of entitlement and dating is no different." I could feel how fast the room tipped towards him as he walked in. Immaculately dressed and well-groomed to go with it, everything about him felt infrangible; his voice, his walk, his way, everything. Even the look in his eye was one that didn't so much as look at me but through me. For a man I'd learn soon enough only to speak in soundbites for Daniel De Haan making an impression was all about entrances and exits.

"If anything it's a reflection of today's capitalistic society. Do we truly want to find lasting love anymore, or are we merely seeking affirmation and acceptance through attractiveness? This is something Gary and I question each and every day". My perspective of him slowly slipping away, this was no politician's answer I said to myself as his rather self-effacing response, so articulately put, sank in.

It was then I began to see what they could where others couldn't. Love was no longer about boy meets girl. It's about a world of people needing to make that connection and have everyone else witness it. It was plain to see, privacy was now a part of our past and that we were living in a world where social acceptance rules with an iron fist.

"Am I the last piece in Gary's puzzle is what you're wondering, am I right?" He was indeed and he knew I knew he knew it. Rather than this mercurial reigning recluse of the online dating scene that I'd begun to paint a picture of, I was now starting to see the integral part Daniel played in all this. He was for want of a better expression, the man behind the man.

Much like his counterpart, he too a former athlete, began to recount how the skills he'd acquired as both a screenwriter and producer in the world of film and television whilst living stateside for the best part of a decade had led him to where he was now - his reflection along with a polished air of authority staring back at me.

By all accounts, it was a chance meeting in the early spring of 2009 that had led both men to this point in our conversation. Only, instead of rummaging around like some tabloid reporter as to how this partnership came about, I instead opted for each man's individual take on the matter of what truly happened and how it came to both men becoming leading authorities on love for the *"me generation"*.

Gary: *I'd love to know what he's told you but I can tell you he was on a date that night. Did he tell you that? Bet he didn't. I was working as part of one of my training weekends and was pretty much wrapping up and* we're in this bar. It's business as usual but I'm watching him out the corner of my eye and I don't care what he says to this day, he was dying.

He's talking and talking...and talking, and bearing in mind knowing him now, Dan never talks but it told me he was seeking her approval in some way. And I remember he kept leaning in which is always a rookie mistake as it shows you're more interested in them than they are in you.

But it was the way she was dressed, he's standing there like he does looking all GQ and that and this was a good looking girl mind but she'd made zero effort which for a date I didn't get.

So I'm thinking to myself I've gotta say something here. Well, I wait until he was at the bar getting his breath back and I make my move all covert and I'm like, "all right?" and I hand him my card. He looks down, reads it and he knows I know, then in this single solitary moment of self realisation he let's out a resigning sounding sigh.

So I remember telling him "up your energy as you're sat down...don't be. Instead talk to her in the corner over there where you're not so on show. And another thing, ask her about the necklace she's wearing. I'll lay money on it, it means something to her". [Laughter ensues with a shrug] I assumed I'd never see him again.

Daniel: *For the record, can I just say he is literally the most ardent admirer of his own voice that man, so I know whatever he's told you is gonna shine the spotlight on him unless he tells the story the way it should* be told. But for what it's worth, I remember being sat there at my desk, phone in one hand, his calling card in the other thinking how can I spin this so that he doesn't think I'm thanking him [laughs] even though I've no reason to be ringing otherwise. And he answers with [impersonates] "Gary Gunn", which wound me up because it was like he was this brand.

I'd googled him the day after obviously and it was all Gary Gunn this...Gary Gunn that and he was, he was this brand name which to be brutally honest actually impressed me not that I'd ever tell him that. Anyway, I answered with Gary Gunn? Daniel De Haan".

My devotion to the day and the questions I sought so many answers to had been matched, outdistanced even by the both of them. It's been said that insecurity and affirmation are the two great narcotics of the 21st century so far and if so then these two appear to have the potential to be its antidote.

Because, listening back on those conversations with each other, the introvert and the extrovert, the blend of their two very different voices sounded something close to an essential truth. After all, it was their synergy that seemed to explain the chemistry between the two of them and why this most unlikely of partnerships had prospered the way it had.

As in a modern media age of so many PR-bred alpha-egos and their all-too-often laundered version of reality, these two were anything but. These two had proved to me to be a breed all of their own and that I had been the one privileged enough to capture it. It was then that it eventually dawned on me…

…I never did press the red 'record' button on that Dictaphone of mine.

Anthony Asquith, leading psychotherapist and renowned author of 'Surviving The Human Zoo', April 2016

Copyright © Social Attraction Ltd. 2016

CONTENTS PAGE

Foreword: 9-15

Introduction

A Power All of Our Own: 21-22

Truth Be Told: 23-24

Creating Our Online Dating Character

Pitching Our Perfect Profile: 25

Surveying Our Scene: 26

Setting Our Scene: 26-27

Your Personal Ingredients: 27-28

Your Perfect Preference: 28-30

Assembling Our Answers #1: 33-36

Assembling Our Answers #2: 37-40

Assembling Our Answer #3: 41-44

Answering Our Own Questions: 47-49

The Secret To Our Story

Subtext To Our Story: 51-53

Stance To Our Story: 55-56

Synchronising Our Story: 59-61

Strategy To Our Story: 63-64

Picture Perfect: 67-72

Putting Our Pictures To The Test: 72-73

The Perfect Picture Resolution: 75-76

Evaluating Our Essentials

Creating With Care: 79-80

Practice Makes Perfect: 81-82

Perfecting Our Potential: 85-86

Putting Our Plans In Place

Making Our Mark 1: 89-91

Modelling Our Messages: 93-95

Making Our Mark 2 – Taking It Offline: 97-98

Time To Talk Numbers: 101-102

Making Our Mark 3 – Taking It To The Telephone: 105-106

Calling Our Confidence: 109-112

Getting It Right The First Time: 115

Keeping Matters Moving: 115-117

Decoding Our Dating: 119-122

Further Resources: 125

Copyright © Social Attraction Ltd. 2016

Testimonials

The Comeback Kid: 127-129

A Stranger In A Strange Town: 131-133

A House Is Not A Home: 135-137

Prologue: 139-142

In Tribute - Martin Culverhouse: 145-146

Copyright © Social Attraction Ltd. 2016

Introduction Our Story - A Power All Of Our Own

From the people we meet in the street, to the countless number of clients that come through our doors, to our long-suffering friends and family, this book has come about as a result of one residing factor - for us as we know it, it is the truth be told.

In this (modern) day and (communication) age, everyone who's anyone has an opinion on online dating so it seems. Be it they're just about to begin, are currently out there online, or have that infamous friend that has "been there, seen it, done it and got the t-shirt" we seem to be faced with a flurry of differing opinions and so-called "facts".

The one question we need answering above all others, however, is whether several peoples' personal experiences in this so-called new age of dating are indeed fact, or whether we need to delve deeper in order to find out the fundamental truths.

After all, the information here in this book is not something we stumbled upon but rather it has been compiled through trial and error, not only from our own experiences, but from others we've worked with who have had the same experiences you too are about to go through.

Anyone one of us anywhere has the opportunity to log onto a dating site, set-up a profile and within a mere matter of moments be sending (as well as receiving) messages to women we have never even met. That in itself is empowering and that's before we even know how to go about it in the best way.

But what if we did?

We believe that when reading this book, right here right now, in the pages that follow we will be able to take the privilege of that power and use it to make the most of any opportunities that are about to come our way.

So whatever walk of life we currently find ourselves in, whether we are working away from home, recently single and back out on "the scene", find ourselves relocating or relaunching our lives all over again, or even merely inexperienced and out there for the first time - if we learn the lessons this book is about to teach us, the power for us to choose as opposed to be chosen is about to become our own.

The Truth Be Told

Who we are is who we are, we cannot change that about ourselves and neither should we, but what we can do is to make the most of ourselves and what we do have.

Since we first began working with online profile writing, in that time the one thing above all else that seems to be at the forefront of any issues that arise, is the fact that we are liable to make the mistake of assuming we can do it on instinct alone and that there is no actual science nor structure to it.

We have found that this could not be more wrong as no matter what our looks, status, or success with dating maybe, doing so online is a whole other skill set.

Fiction – There's no science to online dating, anyone can do it.

Fact – When online dating we need the right strategy to get the right results

Whether we want to portray ourselves as a comedian in order to a make a girl laugh, or paint a picture of us in our workplace owning the show; in terms of playing the part our list goes on and on.

What we have found however, is that it is one thing having that one profile that stands out amongst all others which garners us the attention we've been craving, but it's a whole other dilemma when those dates are finally in the diary, and we are the ones walking into the room as we really are.

After following countless clients of ours throughout their entire online dating journey, ultimately what we have learned is that rather than telling female online daters what they want to hear, a far better strategy is to create and construct a profile that captures us as the individual we are; so that when we finally walk through that door and into that all important first date our virtual self will match our actual self.

And never more so than if she has first taken the time to read what we have written in regard to our own personal profile and been captivated enough to want to meet us in person. The next section of our book, demonstrates just how to do that…

Creating Our Online Dating Character – Pitching Our Perfect Profile

Attraction at times can be a complex and confusing concept to comprehend. It does not always add up or make sense for that matter but what it does do is enable us to play to our strengths as men.

Many of us make the mistake of thinking that the best way into a woman's mind is to ask another woman. However, as hard to grasp as this may be, women differ from men for a reason otherwise we would all be the same in this world.

Fiction - I'll get a girl friend of mine to write my profile; she will know what to write to attract girls more than I would.

Fact - Opposites attract for a reason

By filling in the questionnaire in the following chapter - here is our chance to make our words come alive containing our unique masculine energy that will subconsciously attract the women that we want into our lives.

Surveying Our Scene

The aim of the next nine questions is to emphasise and establish the power of attraction already there inside of us. Not only that, but if we automatically answer with the first thoughts and feelings that enter our heads, then who we truly are will without doubt shine through.

Setting Our Scene

1. **Extending Your Ego – Looking back on your life, what is the one thing about you that makes you who you are?**

Through a woman's eyes, by answering this as our opening statement, we're capturing the very essence of what it is that makes us who we are in a way that easily translates on the page and sets the scene for the woman reading all about us.

Answer: My ability to…

2. **One Line Pitch – Define your ideal of who you think a man should be?**

The reason our answer to this question is so important to a woman, is because if we know who we are as a man then that conveys to her the exact same thing which ultimately is what she is searching for.

Answer: Someone who…

3. **Asking Your Own Question – What do you think women want?**

To a woman, by answering this question, no matter which way we do, we cannot escape the fact that we are shining a reflection of our strongest attributes on to her in terms of what we can offer as a man.

Answer: I believe…

Your Personal Ingredients

1. **Home – If something special happens in your life, who is the first person you call and why?**

When a woman reaches this next stage of our profile, it indicates she is ready to discover more about us, therefore how we answer this question is one that will offer her a direct insight into the deeper more personal side of our life.

Answer: My…

2. **Work – Why do you choose to do the job you do?**

This question offers us the opportunity to translate to a woman, what makes us tick as men on a day-to-day basis, showing a side to us that its not so much what we do but rather why we do it.

Answer: Because…

3. **Play – What one thing do you enjoy most in life and why?**

Women when reading what we write in answer to this, will automatically understand what it is that goes beyond getting us up in the morning and will capture in her mind's eye us in our pursuit of happiness.

Answer: I love…

Your Perfect Preference

1. **Your Sweet – What is your dream personality in a girl in 3 words?**

As a man, having the assertiveness to state in words the exact personality traits of our ideal woman, portrays an inner confidence in ourselves that we believe in our own ability to be worthy of what we want.

1…………………………..2…………………………..3……………………..

2. **Your Sour – What is your nightmare personality in a girl in 3 words?**

Our answer to this question is actually our most crucial as what it does is automatically elevate our own value from a woman's perspective demonstrating that we do indeed have a choice over who we decide to date.

1……………………..2……………………….3……………………..

3. **Answering Your Own Question – What do you want a woman to feel when they read your profile and why?**

Having now read our profile, answering this final question as a closing statement is what will allow us the chance to lead a woman so that having evoked the right emotions, she subconsciously will want to follow and find out more about us.

Answer: I would love them to….

Now that we have all nine answers to all nine of our questions, the next step is to collate them in order, to form a coherent and complete profile.

And, if we understand and apply this above method, it will enable us to separate ourselves from the rest with our best profile showing us in our best light.

Three examples of exactly how to do this can be found outlined in the following section.

Notes...

Assembling Our Answers #1

Charlie came to us late last year having made the decision that he needed to take advantage of the holiday season that was fast approaching. Between work and play this was his most social time of year, however, despite always being gung ho and happy go-lucky when it came to trying to win women over, he was also well aware that his antics could often come across as him trying far too hard.

Setting Your Scene

1. **Extending Your Ego** – Looking back on your life, what is the one thing about you that makes you who you are?

My dad always telling me 'you can do ANYTHING you set your mind to' and 'reach for the stars'

2. **One Line Pitch** – Define your ideal of who you think a man should be?

Confident and don't care what anyone else thinks.

3. **Asking Your Own Question** – What do you think women want?

Able to protect and provide.

Your Personal Ingredients

1. **Home – If something special happens in your life, who is the first person you call and why?**

My best friend Matt. Because we speak all the time and share everything

2. **Work – Why do you choose to do the job you do?**

It's something I am passionate about. To help other people and for me to get better myself.

3. **Play – What one thing do you enjoy most in life and why?**

I love self improvement

Your Perfect Preference

1. **Your Sweet – What is your dream personality in a girl in 3 words?**

Outgoing, Mischievous, Confident

2. **Your Sour – What is your nightmare personality in a girl in 3 words?**

Shy, High maintenance, Negative

3. **Answering Your Own Question – What do you want a woman to feel when they read your profile and why?**

I would love them to be Excited and intrigued... they want to know more

Assembled Answer #1

My belief is that you can do anything that you set your mind to and reach for the stars, I'd consider myself confident and not too fussed about what anyone else thinks about me, and I'm wondering whether all women are really after is a man to protect and provide for them?

I'm really close to my friends and I have one in particular who I speak with a lot, I'm lucky enough to do a job that I'm passionate about and help other people too, as well as myself. Yes personal development is important to me.

I'm looking for a girl who is outgoing, mischievous and confident and I'm not really interested in a girl who is shy, high maintenance or negative about life. You should contact me if you were excited and intrigued when you read my profile and want to know more.

Assembled Outcome #1

In the wake of working alongside us and having met a match online shortly after the New Year's celebrations, Charlie is currently celebrating his 6th month anniversary by climbing Mount Inverness in the Scottish highlands with his girlfriend who being an avid climber introduced him what is now their favourite joint hobby.

Assembling Our Answers #2

Richard plucked up the courage and picked up the phone to us when he and his long term girlfriend finally called it quits after more than 5 years of living together. Rather than making the mistake of hiding away from the world, he was adamant that he wanted to try his luck dipping his toe into the online dating pool as way of building himself back up after so long.

Setting Your Scene

1. Extending Your Ego – Looking back on your life, what is the one thing about you that makes you who you are?

My sensitive and emotional nature.

2. One Line Pitch – Define your ideal of who you think a man should be?

Someone who is kind, smart and powerful.

3. Asking Your Own Question – What do you think women want?

Fun

Your Personal Ingredients

1. Home – If something special happens in your life, who is the first person you call and why?

It depends on the nature of the event. But I guess parents because I feel they know me better than I know myself.

2. Work – Why do you choose to do the job you do?

Because it's a combination of art and visuals, which sum up my mixed traits.

3. Play – What one thing do you enjoy most in life and why?

I love drama and atmosphere, so the theatre draws me into another world that feels real and powerful.

Your Perfect Preference

1. Your Sweet – What is your dream personality in a girl in 3 words?

Kind, Happy, Witty

2. **Your Sour – What is your nightmare personality in a girl in 3 words?**

Materialistic, Selfish, Spoiled

3. **Answering Your Own Question – What do you want a woman to feel when they read your profile and why?**

Intrigued and amused.

Assembled Answer #2

My belief is that my sensitive and emotional nature leads me to be someone who is kind, smart and powerful, and I'm wondering whether women just want a man who is a lot of fun?

I'm really close to my family and believe that they know me better then myself, and I'm also lucky enough to do a job which combines my love of art and visuals, which I also feel sums up my mixed personality traits. I'm also a massive fan of drama; the atmosphere at the theatre draws me into another world that feels real and powerful.

I'm looking for a girl who is kind, happy and witty, and I'm not really interested in a girl who is materialistic, selfish, and spoiled. You should contact me if you were intrigued and amused when you read my profile and want to know more.

Assembled Outcome #2

Realising the difference between the man he once was when in his relationship compared to the man he had become since working with us and venturing to date online, Richard in his own words describes his new-found confidence as a "revelation". So much so that having been apart for the best part of a year, Richard and his ex-girlfriend following a chance meeting have made the move to try again.

Assembling Our Answer #3

Marcus was a man who had found himself to be single for most of his adult life as he travelled the majority of time due to his work. Personable in his approach yet never one to make the first move when it came to the opposite sex, he had found himself somewhat frustratingly always being on the outside of his social life looking in.

Setting Your Scene

1. Extending Your Ego – Looking back on your life, what is the one thing about you that makes you who you are?

My ability to adapt to any social situation and make others feel comfortable

2. One Line Pitch – Define your ideal of who you think a man should be?

Someone who is genuine has strength of character and knows when to be firm or romantic but always fair and with a sense of humour.

3. Asking Your Own Question – What do you think women want?

I believe despite the pressure for women to be everything a man is and more, that ultimately women want to be respected, listened to, loved, cherished and romanced whilst having a lot of fun and trying out new things.

Your Personal Ingredients

1. Home – If something special happens in your life, who is the first person you call and why?

My best mate as we have shared many ups and downs over the years and always back each other up.

2. Work – Why do you choose to do the job you do?

Because it's a lifelong passion of mine to help get the best out of any individual and I won't rest until my business reaches millions of people.

3. Play – What one thing do you enjoy most in life and why?

Travelling to new places and new experiences is a real passion but my family and close friends are what it's really all about.

Your Perfect Preference

1. Your Sweet – What is your dream personality in a girl in 3 words

Funny, intelligent, sexy.

2. Your Sour – What is your nightmare personality in a girl in 3 words?

Egotistical, stupid, without humour

3. Answering Your Own Question – What do you want a woman to feel when they read your profile and why?

I would love them to realise that whilst having a lot of fun that old fashioned values, chivalry and romance are still very much alive and it's not at the expensive of a woman's intelligence or ambition.

Assembled Answer #3

I believe that my ability to adapt to any social situation and make others feel comfortable makes me someone who is genuine, has strength of character and knows when to be firm or romantic, but always fair and with a good sense of humour.

I believe despite the pressure for women to be everything a man is and more, that ultimately women want to be respected, listened to, loved, cherished and romanced and I'm wondering whether what women really want is a lot of fun, and an opportunity to try out new things?

I'm really close to one friend in particular; we have shared many ups and downs over the years, and have always been there to back each other up.

I'm lucky enough to work in an area that is a lifelong passion of mine, with my aim being to get the best out of any individual.

Travelling to new places and gaining new experiences is a real passion of mine, but my family and close friends are what it's really all about.

I'm after a woman who is funny, intelligent and sexy, and I'm not interested by a girl who is egotistical, stupid and without humour. You should contact me if you realise that whilst having a lot of fun that old fashioned values, shivery and romance are still very much alive and it's not at the expensive of a woman's intelligence or ambition.

Assembled Outcome #3

Having taken to the online dating pool literally like a fish to water, Marcus now divides his time between home and abroad as due to our one-on-one guidance that he credits us with, dates on a regular basis wherever he happens to be in the world.

Having now put the pieces of the puzzle together to form our own online dating character, we can clearly see that it portrays us in our best light, and also offers an invaluable insight into the exact type of women that we would like to attract into our lives.

All in all, a powerful profile written the right way forms the sole basis to all of our online dating success.

Notes...

Answering Our Own Questions - FAQ 1 - What dating site should I use?

There are countless different dating sites from which to choose from, so much so that it can be hard to know just which one is the best one for you. Our advice is to try out and use three different dating sites simultaneously.

The most successful result we have found from our clients is when they choose one free site such as pof.com, a leading site with which they pay a subscription such as singleswarehouse.com plus a niched site which will target them more specifically such as uniformdating.com.

The reason as to why we suggest trying three sites at the same time is so that we are able to alter and adjust our profile in order to test out and try to obtain the best results all round.

The reality is once we have found the right site as a result of refining our profile, if we're ever faced with being single ever again, we will know the exact right site to use with the exact right profile to use for it.

Plus, with an entire three dating profiles live online and all at the same time, we are in actual fact making ourselves three times more likely to meet the woman we want as opposed to solely relying on just one profile to do all the work.

FAQ 2 - Having filled out the questionnaire, I feel like my profile could be worded better what can I do?

If you feel that your profile could be refined more then we offer a professional writing service which can be found on our website **www.socialattraction.co.uk**

We offer professional profile rewrites through to full online dating packages.

FAQ 3 - Is there any way in which I can get my profile to be viewed online by more women more often so I don't have to spend as much time myself online?

Yes, there is. We have come to realise that if we update part of our profile on a daily basis, this will enable us to be placed right at the top of the search rankings when women run their search.

All we need to do is simply change full stop for a comma for example or change a word and this will automatically update our profile renewing its status as new. This is because online dating sites like to put the most active profiles near the top of their search engines that women will run. This way we can maximise our potential for women to contact us first.

It's also highly beneficial for us to run a search on women daily as any new female members will be the most keen to make contact in order to meet someone so attempt to message them as soon as possible.

FAQ 4 – There are other dropdown boxes which I need to fill in and answer on my profile, have you any advice on how to handle these?

Yes, our research indicates that men who include the following information on their dating profiles receive more attention online:

- Men looking for a serious relationship.

- Men who have been in a relationship for 4 years or more.

- Men over 6ft tall.

- Men who earn over £100K a year.

Another main area that many men slip up on is by selecting an age range of a potential partner far too young compared to their own. We have found that men whose age range of a potential partner is the same as their own or within being 10 years younger achieves the best success when online dating.

The Secret To Our Story - Subtext To Our Story

Now we have reached the stage of having written our own online dating profile, more often than not the majority of dating sites out there will follow on from this with a few added questions that you will need to answer and include.

It is at this important point that we have the chance to word our answers in a way that not only entices the women reading it, but also allows them the opportunity to easily email us to find out more.

Fiction – When asked, we should aim to answer all questions when online dating directly.

Fact – Using the art of mystery entices women to want to know more about us.

Now it's time for us to cultivate the meaning of mystery in order to generate attention from women online by answering questions in an intriguing way they wouldn't ever have experienced before.

Example Answer #1: Favourite local hot spots or travel destinations?

A standard answer would be:

"I love visiting Brazil and go there as often as I can."

Instead, answer it as:

"Certain parts of South America I cannot get enough of and it's the culture that keeps drawing me back there for more."

Why?

By being vague about the exact location in South America allows women an easy opportunity to ask us specifically where and what kind of culture we like.

Example Answer #2: What I'm doing with my life?

A standard answer would be:

"Working a lot during the week and trying to make the most of my weekends."

Instead, answer it as:

"I'm too busy living it to be thinking about it."

Why?

The subtext here conveys that we are indeed a busy individual leading a full life whilst also not giving the game away which implies an element of mystery.

Example Answer #3: Tell us more about your job?

A standard answer would be:

"I'm a primary school teacher who loves working with kids who also loves the long holidays in between."

Instead, answer it as:

"Every day I wake up I can honestly say I follow my passion, and whilst some would consider it maybe mundane, for me I chose this path because despite knowing my limits I like to push myself to them."

Why?

Because essentially what we're doing here is explaining our emotions and how we feel about our job which demonstrates what it means to us and the positive effect it has on our life but without giving the game away so again they're left wanting more.

Stance To Our Story - FAQ 1 – I'm not too comfortable being mysterious, it's just not who I am as a person, what can I do?

What we need to try and remember about online dating is that it is simply a platform to put single men and women together, and as such, our strategy must be to make our profile stronger in order to stand out more. This will ultimately make it easier for women to contact us and as a result make it more likely to make dates to go on.

And so, being mysterious is considered an incredibly powerful way of generating female attention when online dating. It is not the only strategy of course, but it is definitely one of the most effective we find.

We always tell our clients to try and think of it like wearing a specific piece of clothing and although we maybe are not completely comfortable wearing that piece of clothing, every time that we do, attractive women approach us and start talking to us more as they find it attractive. If this were the case, should we wear the item or not? Of course we should and it's no different from when we are creating mystery about ourselves online in order to generate more female attention.

FAQ 2 – How vague is too vague when answering these questions?

If we look at the examples that we are given here, rather than being specific by stating a job title for example, we have left that out and instead opted to talk about the emotions of what our job makes us feel and what it means to us. Again, another example is rather than talking specifically about Brazil, instead we spoke about South America as a whole. Remember less is more.

The key to being mysterious is to write what we would like to say and then to take out any and all of the definitive areas, making what we say much more vague. This then leaves matters open for further discussion and makes it far easier for a woman to want to contact us because they merely want to know more. In other words, the more general we are the more specific they'll be.

Notes...

Synchronising Our Story

Recently, we have come to realise that one of the resounding reasons why we sometimes struggle to get the results online that we so desire is due to the fact that there is an inconsistency in the correlation between our username, logline, profile pictures and story.

We have found that each one of these individually is important but when constructing a profile, to maximise its potential, the more cohesive each of these are together the stronger your chances of the right results are.

Fiction: Our username and logline are not important.

Fact: Our username, logline and photos form a woman's first impression of us.

Now the time is right for us to synchronise our own online dating story.

Example Username and Logline

Having the right username and logline will speak for itself in terms of introducing your online dating character to the online dating world.

Bad Example #1: Hotstuff0181, Logline: Once Bitten, twice shy, third time lucky

Rather than subtly implying it, this username falls into the trap of trying too hard in that its telling you he's the best and that's he knows he's attractive, which in itself is unattractive.

This log line is a prime example of an online dater trying to be clever without really thinking about what it is he's conveying, as he is sub-communicating that he does not get much attention online which is hardly enticing to a woman.

Bad Example #2: Username: Downesy1234 Logline: Let's give this a try

The username is demonstrating both a lack of imagination and effort which implies a lazy attitude.

The logline is conveying a lack of confidence that as a first impression is unattractive.

Bad Example #3: Username: buckle, Logline: Hmm this again…

This nondescriptive username is a reflection of a nondescriptive personailty.

This logline shows a negative pattern forming in that if he's back online again it shows his last relationship did not work out which implies that he's not a long term potential partner to date.

Good Example #1: Username: Mr_Brightside, Logline: It started out with a click

Straight away we can see that this user's profile has not only started to paint a picture of his personality from the start but that clearly he is a music lover which will resonate with his perfect partner.

Good Example #2: Username: National Velvet, Tagline: Reign me in

Straight out of the gate, we can tell that this user's profile is a racing lover and with his logline he knows how to subtly flirt too.

Good Example #3: Username: Music_Maker, Logline: Addicted to love

The great thing about this is that it is what it says on the label and that immediately we know that not only is he a music lover but a romantic to go with it.

Each of these examples only go to show the power of congruency and how paramount it is in terms of painting a picture of ourselves when putting ourselves out there into the online dating world.

Strategy To Our Story - FAQ 1 – I'm finding that all of the good usernames are taken so what should I do?

This is simple for us to solve. If there is a name that we want only its already been taken already, for example MrBrightside, what we can then do is to add in an underscore _ character between the words to so that it still reads the same way yet has only changed in terms of its appearance. In other words it has become Mr_Brightside but if this is still an issue then we can try taking out the capital letters instead so that it reads mr_brightside.

Either way it is best to avoid adding any irrelevant numbers and/or characters that don't need to be there, or have any meaning exactly. And following on from that, if we really are unable to get the username we want to work then its best to come up with a whole new username and one that is easier to make work for us.

FAQ 2 – I really can't think of a good username and logline to come up with what can I do?

We suggest looking at names of song titles or the titles of movies as an easy way of finding usernames and loglines that fit with who we truly are. Basically anything that you are interested in as a person be it fashion, films, songs or sport etc, choose something that resonates with you.

After all, we are painting a picture online of who we are so we must make sure that our profile is totally congruent with who we are and at the same time sends that same message.

Notes…

Picture Perfect

The final piece of the congruency puzzle as we like to call it is to make sure that the personal photos we choose to complement our profile are picture perfect. The main aim of this is so that we can easily convey in each single shot the differing sides of us that make up our persona. After all, they say a single picture can say more than a thousand words ever could – well here is our chance to put it into practice.

The Headshot

This is the all important opening visual, the first photo a woman will see that is supposed to say so much about us and most crucial of all, forms the first impression of us in terms of attraction. Therefore, from our choice of clothing and hairstyle to the correct location and lighting, again, congruency on camera in terms of the style we keep is the most important part of our profile.

Below are two examples each of headshots recommended and taken via professional photographer Saskia Nelson founder of the studio Saturday Night's Alright who specialise in online dating photography.

Example photo one:

What makes this picture a perfect one is the fact that he has set his scene in an ideal environment. It tells us that he enjoys the outdoors and that the way he dresses style wise, implies that he is a "relaxed fit" in terms of his personality.

Example photo two:

This headshot here is ideal as both the lighting and (*black & white*) tone captures the man's mood, making him the centre of attention in terms of the commanding presence he portrays.

The Action Shot

The key to these images is for us to use a picture portraying ourselves in action whilst participating in activities that we have a passion for taking part in. This can mean anything from a sports related pastime such as skiing or martial arts to playing an instrument as being in part of a band but whatever it is, it must capture us in the moment doing what it is we love to do so that whoever's looking can catch a glimpse into our life as we live it.

Example photo one.

This action shot here is ideal as it frames the man in the moment. It represents him in his element performing stand up comedy which conveys not only a humorous and intelligent element to his personality but it implies both confidence and a commanding presence – two equally attractive personality traits to the opposite sex.

Example photo 2

This action shot is a prime example of a man who has set his scene in terms of who he is.

From one simple shot we can depict who he is (a man not afraid to display his passion) and what he represents (yoga promotes both a depth of character and spiritual understanding) which is what you want when you are dating online.

The Social Shot

The idea behind an ensemble shot such as this is to portray the way that we socially lead a healthy life to match a healthy lifestyle. The more friends we include means the more fun we are having. And that the less posed the picture that we take here will mean the more natural we will come across.

Example photo 1

This example of a social shot is a picture perfect representation of how to come across on a public forum.

From its black & white artistically classical tone to it bright lighting that lightens its mood and enhances the humour, every one of the men in this shot proves themselves an ideal candidate for a fun day out in their fanciest attire.

Example photo 2

This social shot is ideal in its simplicity. From its surrounding setting of the bar to the closeness of the compatriots who are posing in the picture, it is a nice natural way of conveying friendship at its finest and implies a fun time had by all that are here.

Putting Our Pictures to the Test

Before we brave choosing the photos we have had taken of us and putting them live online along with our new dating profile, we must first and foremost test them in terms of gaining feedback.

This testing is carried out via the use of a dating app titled Tinder or a similar dating platform which ultimately relies on the use solely of photos in order to select a match.

If we register ourselves on Tinder and upload the three shots of us that have been suggested and then further more swipe yes to around approx 100 women who we find attractive, then depending on what response rate we get will depend on how effective our photos are – the more matches the more successful we will know our photos to be.

We have found through a matter of extensive trial and error that clients who have used this process in the past have had a far higher response rate online than clients who have only sought feedback from their friends and family.

When all is said and done, this has so far proven to make the process of online dating that much simpler.

All in all the aim and objective of our profile, username, logline and photos is to send the same congruent message to the female readers of our profile that creates our unique online dating character in their head, that they are only too keen to want to meet in person.

The Perfect Picture Resolution - FAQ 1 – I'm not getting any matches on Tinder or any other mobile apps that are based on appearance alone, is there anything I do?

There is an array of different ways in which we can increase our matches on mobile dating apps, such as making our photos black and white or even sepia toned. Only using one photo instead of three or even wearing a hat tilted at an angle to distinguish oneself.

If we find ourselves still struggling then one way we have had great success with is having clients have professional photos taken of themselves. Just be sure to let the photographer know what the photo is for exactly, so that they know how to best bring out our most attractive qualities.

FAQ 2 – I'm really not photogenic enough, what can I do?

We have found that certain dating sites allow users to use an artist's impression of themselves as opposed to using real life photographs.

If we truly feel that we are not anywhere near photogenic enough, then it's best to choose a dating site that allows us to use these kinds of caricatures and then find an artist that can draw us in a rather more charming way.

After all, having an artist's impression of ourselves, allows us to stand out from the crowd when women are running searches for their matches for men.

Notes…

Evaluating Our Essentials - Creating With Care

Sometimes it is the little things in life that seem to make the biggest difference, especially with regards to our online dating profiles, in that we can take various aspects of it for granted too much of the time..

Countless clients of ours come to us complaining that meeting women "out and about" isn't an issue for them so why when online are they finding themselves falling short? And the answer more often than not is that it's the minor mistakes that they make that are letting them down more than anything else, hence, why we always hit home that fundamentals come first.

Fiction – A few mistakes here and there when it comes to punctuation, grammar or spelling won't matter.

Fact – Any mistakes when it comes to punctuation, grammar or spelling here, there or anywhere will put women off.

Naturally, it may sound like common sense but more often than not it is the simple little things that are overlooked the most.

Just like when we were taught in English class all about punctuation, grammar and spelling the same still holds up today so we must remember to carry out a simple spell-check and proof read as it will reap us rewards in the long run.

At the same time we must remind ourselves that we are not texting but online dating and that yes, there is a difference, a massive one in fact. Therefore, we must ensure never ever to use texted abbreviations whilst online.

After all, no matter how minor, attention to detail is what will separate our profile from the rest.

Practice Makes Perfect

With this being the communication age and as a result everything in our day-to-day lives in general becoming somewhat quicker and easier, online dating is proving no different.

Once upon a time, we had singles ads in the newspaper which eventually became online dating websites which now are becoming mobile phone apps. It's as much a part of technical evolution as it is a physical one.

Many clients come to us with the misconception that using an online dating mobile phone app is the smartest move to make. They literally spend countless hours of the day surfing and searching out new users, answering back to replies and approaches and notifications almost immediately, whilst generally indicating that they are "currently online" all day long. Here lies the problem.

Fiction – Using an online dating app makes my life so much easier.

Fact – Using an online dating app conveys you have nothing better to do with your time which in itself is unattractive.

Following on from this, we must make use of our new found discipline and give ourselves a window of one hour per day for no less than ninety days.

In that one hour we must make sure to carry out all of our messages for that day and if we do happen to run over then we simply carry them over to the next day.

Becoming a creature of habit in this scenario will strongly serve its purpose by building a structure that will enable you to put building blocks in place in terms of online dating on a regular basis, the right way.

Notes…

Perfecting Our Potential - FAQ 1 – Can I still use the app even if I only log on for an hour a day?

We have found dating apps to be the cause of countless issues with regards to getting good results online. Besides, even when we are logged out of an app it will still alert us to give a notification, and let's be honest, curiosity will always get the better of us.

Ultimately, the more active and online we are, the less in line we fall with maintaining that mysterious high value strategy/profile we have been putting into practice.

FAQ 2 – 90 days seems a rather long time, must I really need to spend 90 hours doing this before I begin to see results?

Online dating is a skill and with skill comes practice. Even with the information included in this book, it will still take us time to refine our own individual style in order to master all those little intricacies and nuances that arise along the way.

That however, is not to say that we won't get the results we want right away just that we should be ready for anything rather.

After all, having now read this book, some of us will meet our partners during our first few days online whereas others of us may take as long as the entire 90 days in which to do so.

Regardless of timeline, the end result is that with 90 hours worth of experience online dating, we will all be in a far better position and with far more know-how as to how best to go about it.

Notes…

Putting Our Plans In Place - Making Our Mark

We all want to feel as though we have made a connection with someone that we seem to match with online. However, in our experience we stand by the fact that less is more when it comes to communicating.

More often than not, clients comes to us asking how we best address the dilemma of them wasting too much time online messaging someone they have met and yet find unable to make a date with.

In a nutshell, our findings have demonstrated that sending no more than 2 messages is the maximum amount of communication you must have before your chances are seriously minimised in terms of getting a date in the diary.

Fiction - The more time that I spend messaging and getting to know her then the more she will like me.

Fact – After the first 2 messages anymore time spent sending e-mails will put you in the friend zone.

Making Our Mark Stage One - The Opening Email

Here is our simplified three step message formula so that we can easily and effectively contact any women of interest:

Step 1 – Flirt

Step 2 – Like

Step 3 – Question

For example here is a message that a 36 year old man sent online.

Hey there,

Firstly, you'll be pleased to know I made it "all the way" to the bottom of your profile which took me all of about 2 seconds!

Step 1 - Flirt – Her profile consisted of only one paragraph therefore allowed us an opportunity to be both fun and flirty.

And I must say, having now read it (jokes aside), I actually do admire a woman that lets her actions speak louder than her words judging from your photos.

Step 2 – Like - Indicate something special about her profile that caught your eye and pay her a genuine compliment and with her it was her photos.

Tell me something, what's your favourite destination in Asia? Mine's Penang, due to the food I fell in love with whilst there.

Step 3 - Question – Pinpoint a part of her profile that you would like her to elaborate on further for you. On this specific profile she had several photos of her travelling around Asia.

Example email #2:

Hey,

French kissing even before the first date...wow! Someone sounds keen ;)

On a serious note though - I'm impressed with the Marilyn Monroe quote, but do tell me ... do you believe chivalry is really dead?

Paul

Modelling Our Messages - FAQ 1- Why is flirting here having to mean picking holes in her profile or picture?

The aim of the "flirting" area of our e-mail messages is to let the women reading our profiles in on the fact that we are fun and interesting and not afraid to make our presence felt. And so to select something about her profile that isn't quite right (if carried out correctly), will come across as charming.

We more than understand that many men struggle to get this part of their message right, therefore, in our experience we find it best to test different ways in which to flirt in order to find our own individual way. Once we get the flirting aspect of our e-mail message right, we will soon see our response rate increase dramatically.

So stick with it and test as many different ways as possible, and don't be too disheartened if you don't get it right first time. Instead, keep a note of the flirting part that does seem to generate a positive reaction/response and build on it from there.

FAQ 2 – I'm not particularly comfortable with the flirting part, can I just leave it out?

In our experience of sending online dating messages, all we can say is that if we were online dating we would include a flirting part in every single message we'd send out, as it makes us stand out from the crowd in terms of the messages women will be receiving on a day-to-day basis.

The end result is that women are receiving the same types of messages from a multitude of men on a daily basis, and so, we have found that including the flirting part of it, separates us from the rest and guarantees that all important positive response.

FAQ 3 - I'm following your first e-mail message exactly as you suggest and I have not received a reply, can I send her another message?

If we have sent a message to someone that we like the look of and they haven't replied to us at all then we would strongly suggest either focusing our attention elsewhere, or instead, send one more message just in case they weren't in a position to reply to our first one.

However, when messaging them again only do so just one more time and wait an entire seven days later before sending. Write a simple flirtatious one instead of using the three step formula as followed in the book. This can include picking out anything in the profile of note be it a bad photo or even a minor spelling error etc – the key here however is to make the flirting aspect more important than our initial message.

FAQ 4 - Can you give me some ideas for a message title as some dating sites require one?

The key to an effective e-mail title online is to use what is known as "trance words". If we read through women's profiles then we will see that they use specific emotional words through their profile to explain themselves.

For example the words passion, love and happiness are used on a regular basis by women when writing their profiles. Therefore, for the perfect title to our message simply select her top three "trance words" and include them in our title.

Making Our Mark Stage Two – Taking It Offline

After we receive a reply to our original stage one message, putting ourselves in a woman's shoes, she's now read our message, our profile, username, logline and seen our pictures - and as a result has more than has a clear idea of who we are by now.

The fact that she has taken the time to reply to our message is a clear indicator that she is in fact interested in us, and so it's time to take that interest and turn it into talking on the telephone.

Here's her reply:

Hey

Wow, Penang that's amazing! Not somewhere I managed to get to but definitely on my list for next time. I've also heard the food is great there too, what was your favourite?

My favourite place was Vietnam as the culture and the people there are truly amazing! Have you ever been?

Louise X

Here is our stage two reply

Hey,

The street food there is my favourite; I absolutely love the wanton mee noodles. I've not managed to get to Vietnam yet, although I have heard great things from friends and family about it.

I don't tend to come online much because I'm working on a new project right now but what's your number as I'll give you a call and we can talk properly.

All in all, this stage two message is about answering any questions that she's posed previously and then confidently cutting to the chase to ask for her phone number.

Notes…

Time To Talk Numbers - FAQ 1 – This all seems so quick, can I not get to know her better first by talking to her on instant messenger instead?

Remember, our number one strategy when online dating is to convey a sense of mystery, and so, as soon as we start logging onto instant messenger in order to talk to them, we also start to lose our mystery too.

We have both read each other's profiles and have sent the other a message already and so sending instant messages is not only a waste of time, but more often than not, a minefield too in terms of us running the risk of ruining the dialogue already taken place and resulting in the ruling out of any potential date that may take place

The aim of online dating is that it is to be used as a platform in order to meet women in real life, and so, too much dialogue will only prevent that from happening, more often than not.

FAQ 2 – Can I not talk to her just for a little longer on the phone so she seems more comfortable?

If we think that, then what we are actually saying is that we are not comfortable enough to ask her out on a date yet. We must have faith in what we are doing and the belief in ourselves enough so that we can back it up.

After all, once we have one woman who wants to go on a date with us, our confidence will be far more making it far easier to get more of these dates in the diary.

Notes…

Making Our Mark Stage Three - Taking it to the Telephone

The main aim of this initial call is so that she can not only hear our voice for the first time but also to put her mind at rest by having her put a voice to the profile as such. We should make sure to keep the call to a maximum of five minutes long, no longer, before we say our goodbyes with the promise of calling her again a few days later in order to organise meeting with her in person.

As an example, call her and simply say, *"I can't talk for long because I'm on my way to the gym"*, or *"I'm just about to meet friends"*, or *"I'm about to go into a meeting"*.

Following on from this, ask her a question or two about herself to switch the focus onto her. For example, ask, *"What have you planned for the rest of the day?"*, or *"So what have you been up to today so far?"*, or *"Any plans for the weekend yet?"*

Then to wrap matters up, as an example, end the call by saying something along the lines of, *"Well let me call you towards the end of the week and we can put a date in the diary"*, or *"let me give you a call early next week and we can work out when it's best to get together"*, or *"I'll telephone you over the weekend to see how your week's looking and we can take it from there"*.

This works well because not only are we not coming across as overly keen by wanting to talk to her too much and for too long, but at the same time we haven't aimed straight for a date from the start which again demonstrates that we live a busy life which in itself is an attractive trait.

As a result, what this does ultimately is pre-frame our potential relationship from the beginning, in that we are leading the entire interaction which implies assurance as well as allowing the attraction and excitement to build between us before meeting in person.

Notes…

Calling Our Confidence - FAQ 1 – I'm not comfortable enough asking her out on the phone can I text her instead?

In all honesty, we have found that as soon as we text a girl it opens up a dialogue between both of us, and that the end result being that we will lose a lot of that all-important mystery that we will have built up and that surrounds us. Therefore, for the time being it is not worth losing.

Calling a woman directly on the phone and organising a date off the back of it demonstrates massive confidence, which will only heighten her expectations of meeting us in person, plus, making it much more unlikely for her to not cancel on us.

FAQ 2 – What if she doesn't answer, should I leave a message or just call her back another time?

We have found that the best strategy is to leave an answer phone message. When we do, try to sound upbeat with enough energy to simply say who we are and then ask her to give us a call back when she is able to.

The aim is to feel confident when we leave the message as this will come across in our tone. Also, if we are expectant that she will call us back when we leave the message then she will be much more likely to.

If we leave a message and she doesn't get back to us however, then we have found it best to move on and continue with our search. In other words do not waste valuable time and energy wondering if she will get back to us, or if we should try to call again. If we've left a message she will receive it, and if she doesn't get back to us then it simply was never meant to be.

FAQ 3 – What happens if she claims she is busy?

If she has given us her number to call her then she is interested in meeting up with us. If she simply says she is too busy then all we do just ask her to give us a call back when she has more time and leave it for her to come back and make the next move.

If she is unable to make the date we suggest then more often than not she will suggest another date herself so to meet up with us. We must not forget that we have a great profile and she is just as keen to meet with us as we are with her.

FAQ 4 - I've followed your structure and am organising a lot of dates as of late and yet I'm getting cancelled on a lot, even when we've been texting and talking all week, only I don't know why?

The reality is that even if the girl is sending us messages and we are keen to meet her, we must stick to our structure and maintain the lead in the interaction. If she is messaging us and we start replying then we have lost control of the situations and now the woman that we like is leading us, and even though this may feel great at the time, the reality is that all the great work that we have done prior to this will be undone.

We will kill the mystery that we have created about ourselves by giving her more information about ourselves over text, we will kill the anticipation of meeting us for the first time by being too available on our mobile phones, and most of all she will likely be bored by the time the date comes around and delay or even cancel the date.

Following this strategy will frame our whole relationship with the woman from the start that we are in control and leading, which is highly alluring.

FAQ 5 – What happens if she wants to follow, connect or friendship request me via social media, what should I do?

The temptation to connect on social media is highly alluring, however in our experience this will instantly kill the mystery that we have built up around ourselves.

Ultimately yes if we date the girl then we will add her to our social media channels, but what we need to remember is that there is a process to dating and giving away everything about us at the touch of a button kills all of the great work that we have done with our profiles.

When we meet a girl there should be this magical moment of anticipation, excitement and not knowing that is going to happen next, rather than questions about our photos on Facebook and posts or tweets that we have written or shared.

Remember we want to be leading the interaction the whole time, so even if a friend request arrives from the girl we have organised to meet, simply hold off on accepting it until we have met her in person and let the interactions progress naturally

Notes…

Getting It Right The First Time

We're standing there, we're looking back at ourselves in the mirror, we're feeling one part excitement, one part anxious and that third and final part pressure - pressure of it wanting to go well, pressure of her liking us as much as we like her but most of all the pressure more importantly of what we're are going to do before we've even done it.

Fiction – I'm lucky enough to land a date with an amazing girl with the looks to go with it, so I know I need to pull out all the stops including dinner as well as drinks.

Fact – Taking a girl for dinner on a first date puts too much strain on both you and her.

Now, it's time for us to take the pressure of the date and make it a fun one to remember.

Keeping Matters Moving

The objective of our first date is to keep matters moving so that the pressure never has a chance to build enough so that the both of us are either bored or worse uncomfortable. Basically the more we move, the more new and improved and therefore relaxed the date will be.

Some examples of great ideas on dates in terms of ways of counteracting this can be found below:

Existing Event – The best impression to give is when we can imply we have an interesting life based upon interests and activities that we can share such as a passion for music resulting in a live gig to go to.

This is where we have the chance to invite any potential date to join us and experience what we experience and makes it much more fun for them to come with us.

At the same time, we will also find it makes them more interested to say yes, especially as the pressure of a date is lessened the more the two of us will interact over something fun to share.

Shopping – We need to buy a new tie for a job interview, well what better way to do so than to seek a woman's opinion and have her help us shop for it. This in turn gives the date a purpose, implies we trust her judgement or value her opinion, not only that, but it also allows us the chance to keep matters moving.

The Mini Date – This is where we take several fun and exciting experiences and as a result, roll them into one. Be it the bowling alley before grabbing a coffee together, a dance or cookery class that leads into a dinner of street food as we take a walk together or say the ice skating rink that leads us into a round or two of crazy golf followed by a comedy night or an evening of wine tasting.

Whatever it is, roll it into one and keep the momentum going by sharing the energy.

Ultimately, any one of these three dates will work well because both us and them will be participating in something not only fun and entertaining but as a result exciting which is the mood any one of us will want to hope for.

This in turn, lessens any strain put upon us by the pressures that a first date can create.

Decoding Our Dating - FAQ 1 – I'm asking myself, what should I talk to a woman about when on a date?

We have found in the past that if we come well equipped with some fun questions to ask a woman when on a date, then the conversation between the two of us is far less likely to become boring or mundane.

Below we have carefully selected a 'best of the best' list compiled of our personal favourites in terms of questions to ask a woman when on a date. Divided into sub categories, we have personally found each and every one of them to not only be entertaining and enticing, but also a great way of truly getting to know whoever we are meeting with.

Music, TV and Film Related Questions.

What would you name your first album if you were a musician?

Which one song would you say does define the soundtrack of your life?

Which TV show did you watch the most from your childhood?

If you could be any superhero, which one would you be?

What superpower would you have if you could have any for 24 hours?

Which celebrity would you most like to swap lives with for the day?

If you could go back and this time be considered a child prodigy, what talent would you most like to have?

If you could write a book what would be its subject matter?

Fun & Engaging Questions.

If a genie granted you three wishes, what would each of them be?

If you were to host a dinner party and invite three people from history, who would you choose and why?

If you had to live your life by a motto what would that motto be?

Living your life so far, what would you consider has been your favourite age?

Which one piece of advice would you give yourself if you could go back and live your life again?

Would you rather apologise after the event or ask permission before?

If you could have any job in the world other than your own, what would it be?

What is the best present that someone has ever given you and who was that person?

If you won the lottery what would you do with your winnings?

Travel Related Questions.

What is the best holiday destination you've ever been to?

If you could travel anywhere in the world where would it be?

If you could live anywhere in the world where exactly would you choose?

FAQ 2 – Can you give me some examples of what you consider to be a bad date to go on and why?

Of course, in fact, simply understanding the difference between going on a good date as opposed to a bad, can help us in planning for a far better time. Below are what we consider the three worst no-go areas to go on for a first date.

Going to the cinema – This may be surprising to some but the cinema is actually a thoughtless first date idea as it involves sitting down in a silent environment without any interaction with one another.

This conveys a complete lack of planning and is also a sign that we are not used to dating as it suggests we're aiming for as little interaction as we can. No, never go to the cinema on a first date, instead we suggest saving this for a later date.

Taking them out for dinner – Dinner has arguably got to be one of the worst first date ideas possible. We not only have to sit opposite each other and eat but equally engage in conversation with the attention on us.

We run the risk of not only feeling uncomfortable in front of the other person but self-conscious at the same time so we strong advise against it. It can also feel like we're sat in an interview which may be too much too soon seeing as we still need to get to know one another first.

Notes…

Further Resources

Our Weekly Blog – Every Friday we publish our latest blog which is full of free dating advice for single men. To sign up for free visit:

www.socialattraction.co.uk

Our YouTube Channel - We publish a brand new video every day which focuses on every single aspect of becoming attractive to women. To subscribe for free visit:

https://www.youtube.com/user/socialattraction1/

Our Podcast – Our Education In Dating Podcast was launched in 2016. We interview men who are extremely successful with women and learn how we can model their behaviours to become more successful ourselves. To sign up for free visit: **www.socialattraction.co.uk**

Our Online Dating Profile Writing Service – If after reading this book you are still not confident enough to write your own online dating profile, then let us write one for you. For more information visit:

http://www.socialattraction.co.uk/online-dating-advice/

Our Live Training – We offer live training weekends where we teach you the fundamentals of how to approach and attract women in real life scenarios. To learn more visit:

http://www.socialattraction.co.uk/live-training/

Testimonials - The Comeback Kid

If ever there was a testimony to prove that it's never too late in life, then Martin Culverhouse is the man to give it. A 57-year-year old father of three, having spent the last three decades building his business empire before turning it into a family business for his children to take over, Martin came to us on what he now calls the "comeback trail".

His former wife having left the family home whilst his children were still in nappies, Martin had lived the majority of their childhoods raising them by himself whilst juggling work which lasted up until his youngest finally left home for university life.

Martin had always lived his life by the mantra that *"family comes first"*, sacrificing so much for so long both at home and at work which in this day and age is something so many of us can relate to. Only, it had left his lovelife something of a distant memory, a part of his past which for a man still so young with so much to offer, was somewhat hard to live with.

"As successful on paper as I'd become, I won't mince my words, I still felt like a failure when it came to women which frustrated me more than anything. I'd spend my evenings walking my dog wondering if I'd ever meet someone ever again".

Fortunately, it was one day whilst confiding in his next door neighbour that hope finally sprang eternal. Recognising that he needed help, Martin's neighbour referred him to Social Attraction having been a former client of theirs himself. It was that referral that was to set about a series of events changing the shape of Martin's future and with it his future happiness.

"I can remember picking up the phone and thinking, this is a gimmick, it's got to be. Bearing in mind I'd been in business for over 30 years and had seen and heard just about every trick in the book. But what I will say was my neighbour was just about one of the luckiest guys in love I knew so if you can't beat'em join'em, Because when I compare it to the pain I went through whilst wondering all that time, I knew I had no choice as if I didn't have the answer then maybe they did".

An initial consultation face-to-face followed and a plan was put in place to begin creating Martin's profile and within a matter of weeks he was up and running with his brand new profile going live online.

Considering Martin's journey to where he now was, he had always considered himself to be a man ready for anything but what he wasn't ready for was the response he was to receive next. Forty messages followed in the first week he was on there. Not only that but women he would only ever dream of dating not too long before were willing to travel from across the country just to come and meet him.

The ironic twist in the tale turned out to be that with the new-found confidence he had gained from making that call and as a result changing his life, Martin whilst at a local business community gathering met a woman by the name of Linda who would go on to be his partner. That was

18 months ago, the two currently reside together living by the British seaside and spend their days after work walking the dog together.

A Stranger in a Strange Town

Alex Taylor was in a place the majority of us have been before. At 26 and with a promising future ahead of him now that his post-graduate studies were finally behind him, he moved all the way to the bright lights and big city of London for work.

A self-confessed "cool kid" all the way through school with a wide friendship group growing up; the same couldn't be said for him now that he suddenly was left feeling like a stranger in a strange town, his friends no longer there to share his world with.

He also found the rat race city life something of a culture shock but his ambition getting the better of him, made the decision to give it a year before deciding if he would settle there or not. And what a year it would turn out to be.

Throwing himself into his new job, Alex soon discovered that the majority of his time was spent mostly in the office, more often than not working late night after night and even on weekends when need be.

Not only that but unlike the popularity he'd experienced so much for so long back home, working in an office full of people mostly at a more mature point in their lives with families of their own to go home to, meant that it was a struggle for him to ever meet anyone of the opposite sex.

"I felt as though the rug had been pulled out from under me to be honest and could feel myself falling further and further down I was that depressed. There I was meant to be living this dream life in London meeting models and going to parties night after night and instead all I did was work, coming home to a place with no one there".

With *Valentines Day* that year becoming just the same as any other on his calendar, Alex made a move that would turn out to mean more than he could ever imagine. He decided to online date but like so many do, made the mistake of rushing in to it all too soon without further thought.

Before long, he was left feeling like this was something of an uphill battle as he blindly went about what he thought was writing the ideal profile and compiling picture perfect photos. Yet, by the end of the month he found himself getting next to no results much to his frustration. It was then he made the decision to do it properly by getting the help he knew he'd now need.

"To make my mark online I knew I had to learn how and considering I'd spent the past 6 months sat in on my own I didn't want to waste another moment. Googling websites I came across 'Social Attraction' and with their help I came to realise what a simple strategy it was to get me the results I was after. Once I got my head around that and stopped beating myself up so much, everything just grew from there…".

They say results speak for themselves and with 5 dates lined up in the first week alone Alex's results more than told him everything he needed to know. A happy man once again and no longer left feeling like a stranger as such Alex is currently dating regularly and loving the London single life and social scene. And as a reward, Alex has just booked next year's Valentine's Day off for a planned trip to Paris now that he has someone to share it with.

A House Is Not A Home

For Paul Nash, life in the last year has been something of a rollercoaster ride. Having worked hard to climb the career ladder and having married his childhood sweetheart, the 41-year was riding on a wave of success beyond anything he'd ever imagined. Until one day last winter the waves came crashing down all around him.

Having been together since their teens, Paul assumed life with his wife would always be this way and barely could remember a time when it wasn't. Only, between the stresses and strains of working so many hours away from the family home to maintain the highflying lifestyle they lived and his wife wanting him to be more of a stay at home house husband, before long cracks began to appear beyond breaking point.

Sadly this would soon turn out to be only the start of his troubles. A devastated and distracted Paul had found himself not only adjusting to life alone but to make matters worse was suddenly called into head office to be told he was being made redundant.

"It was a nightmare for me. I remember walking through the front door of my so-called dream home, our dream home which we'd bought off the back of my dream job. I literally closed the curtains there and then and hid away I was so rock bottom".

Inside and out Paul no longer recognised the man he saw in the mirror. He decided joining a gym was the one thing he could do to stay sane under the circumstances and give himself a structure to help get his life back on track. And it was whilst working out one day that fate would play in a part in changing his fortune.

"Hearing me talk about my troubles, my personal trainer suggested I join him at a business networking event as he thought it might open a few new doors workwise. It did but not only that, I met the Social Attraction team which seriously sorted me out!"

With a new job opportunity arising from the networking event, all that was left was his love life to address and with the help of Social Attraction, that too soon fell in line with Paul's new persona.

"I caught on quick that confidence was key for me and even though I could barely remember what it was like to date let alone date online. Thanks to Social Attraction I soon found myself going on an average of about two dates per week which was just what I needed to find that confidence inside myself again".

However, not long after Paul found himself widening his social circle and dipping his toe back into the dating pool that an unexpected call came from out of the blue by his wife.

Bridges soon began to be built and this time being different between them both, slowly but surely the pair of them began to grow close again and agreed on giving things another try.

Finally, Paul and his wife are back once again living in their dream home together and with his new job enabling him to remain at home much more often, are currently planning on renewing their wedding vows this coming Christmas. *"If it weren't for Social Attraction giving me my confidence back I maintain to this day that I'd never be back to where I am now".*

Prologue

"Just keep one thing in mind," we both thought but didn't need to say as soon as that tape recorder had been turned off for the final time *"we may remember this all differently by the time it's all over."*

It was just over eighteen months ago that we first made the move to document our findings in the form of a book. Seeing it as an oasis in the midst of male romance's dying embers, the people around us from our families, our friends and our clients helped catapult our persistent and positive hopes into what you've finally read here on the pages in front of you – a mirror image of where we are at in terms of dating in the modern world.

Or in short, we believed we had to orchestrate and present a solid case against the 21st century school of thought that *"romance is dead"*.

Originally, what motivated us most when the time to write arrived during a stifling summer in 2014 was to demonstrate how any one of us could achieve our greatest success through surviving our greatest failure whilst dating online in the 21st century. From the first word of that first line of our opening chapter, that was back then, the only destination of our original journey.

However, what started out as two guys against the (online dating) world, we soon realised as we began to embark upon our research was that what we were representing let alone battling against was something so much more - something not just personal to us but personal to so many other men like us of our generation, of any generation.

The exploration now if you will, was one of a journey of a man somehow out to complete himself. And that, that last piece of the puzzle, the piece that was missing, the piece so many men were out there in search of whether they admitted it or not, was love.

On reflection, all these case studies, clients and many months on, where we've arrived at in terms of telling our story is with a tale told far more touchingly than either of us ever felt we would have when we entered into it. If anything, it seems as if we have written this book a number of times in a number of different ways but having reached the end what we can say with our hand on our heart, is that it is what it is. And that is because through the epic highs, lows and plateaus we ourselves have lived and breathed each and every line.

Day after day we'd interview, and ask question after question of ourselves and of others until the answers somehow came about. All around us were real-life examples of men who thanks to us (so they'd say) had somehow found that ever elusive missing piece of the puzzle. And as a result, word after word we wrote, each and every hallowed page one after the other until it felt like what we had was a happy ending - the kind you read in a book.

Eighteen months later, it was…

How we'd gotten to this point we weren't so sure, in one big burst of belief it had all come together, here we had this untitled, 80,000 word manuscript which made us feel like the world was in our hands. What we had here was an homage to what we believed in when almost everyone else wouldn't. This was our victory lap.

We even showed it to Martin Culverhouse, a man who had been not our first but certainly our favourite client and who we insisted deserved pride of place on the pages within. However, half expecting him to berate us for laying bare his story as well as his soul so openly, we still talk about that one autumn evening when we were handed the phone only to hear his voice, our hands clamming as he spoke.

"Boys, its Martin, Martin Culverhouse" he said as if we didn't know. *"I've read that manuscript of yours"* he followed with a somewhat pregnant pause...

"Publish every word."

We'd reached the end of our journey, having arrived at a destination which the entire time had felt like we'd been trying too hard to hit a bull's-eye, only we hadn't even hung up a target. What did we know?

In truth the moral of ours and everyone else's story turned out to be a simple fact about life itself. And that is, in this so-called communication age in which we live in, all the gimmicks and the gadgetry so accessible at the touch of our fingertips will come and before long go, only to be replaced by more new and improved carbon copies. But it's the fundamentals, the fundamentals to feel, to touch, to tell someone in the flesh what they mean to them in that moment or any other, no matter how raw or rare that may be for the majority of us is what will still stand the test of time.

The timelessness of mastering the art of simple communication between man and woman or when boy meets girl is everybody's birthright, and therefore, will always prove to be something so advanced, so accelerated, so superior that no amount of software or statistics shall ever replace its place in reality.

And so with those closing words we first thought of as we turned that tape recorder off for the final time, now moving from the back to the front of both our minds, the way we remember it was exactly the way it was.

As that's the way life is…

MARTIN CULVERHOUSE: 1956-2016

They say they don't make'em like they used to, we said they were wrong. Martin Culverhouse proved us right…

Charming, disarming and with an unstinting sense of humour, Martin was a shining example of how to make the most of living each and every day. Larger than life, from parent to pillar of the community he had this way of making everyone around him be at ease.

With that wicked smile, unshakeable determination and a sincere care and concern for others, Martin would see himself as an old school gent and insisted everyone else do the same.

A success in all but every area of his life, there was no ego, no entourage and no attitude only his incredible spirit and an insatiable lust for life. One can say this about so few but the man was a true class apart, that rare creation of both a ruthless business man but more importantly a good man.

Learning of his passing in the wake of this book being published there is that point where for us feelings go beyond words. But what we do feel and what we can say is that our careers, our lives were better for him being in them.

Never feeling the need nor seeing the point of explaining himself, he was his own man, a man who to be around him had this way of making you realise you were in the presence of somebody who knew what they were doing.

For two young men making their way in this world that went a long, long way - which is why for us, something of an era has ended.

After all, sometimes in life the way the universe works, it introduces those of us lucky enough to great men.

We are honoured to say Martin Culverhouse was one of them…

Printed in Great Britain
by Amazon